David plec

A book of 30 Bible readings and notes
to help you worship and pray

Tony Phelps-Jones

Published by Scripture Union, 207–209 Queensway, Bletchley, MK2 2EB, England.
Email: info@scriptureunion.org.uk
Internet: www.scriptureunion.org.uk

First published in 2008
ISBN 978 1 84427 308 9

Causeway Prospects is a division of Prospects for People with Learning Disabilities and their address is 69 Honey End Lane, Reading, RG30 4EL. Phone 0118 9516 978. Email: causeway@prospects.org.uk
Website: www.prospects.org.uk

About Causeway Prospects: Causeway Prospects provides resource materials and training to equip churches for effective outreach and ministry among people with learning disabilities. It also runs holiday weekends and special ministry at Spring Harvest and the Keswick Convention.

British Library Cataloguing-in-Publication Data: a catalogue record for this book is available from the British Library.

Cover design by David Lund Design: www.davidlund-design.com

Internal page layout by Creative Pages: www.creativepages.org.uk

Printed and bound in Singapore by Tien Wah Press

Scripture Union is an international charity working with churches in more than 130 countries providing resources to bring the good news about Jesus Christ to children, young people and families – and to encourage them to develop spiritually through the Bible and prayer. As well as a network of volunteers, staff and associates who run holidays, church-based events and school Christian groups, we produce a wide range of publications and support those who use our resources through training programmes.

Using this book

David pleased God and the other titles in this series are intended to help you to worship and pray. On each page there is a reading from the Bible, some thoughts and a prayer.

The readings are from the *Easy-to-Read Version* (ETRV), a very clear and simple translation of the Bible. The reading printed each day is quite short. A longer reading is also given if you would like to read more using your own Bible. There is a list of key words and their meanings near the back of the book.

Reading the Bible

The Bible, which is sometimes called the Word of God, is not really one book but a whole library of many books. The 66 books were written by many people who God spoke to at different times. At the front of the Bible you will find a list of the titles of all the books in the Bible and the page number where each book begins.

To help you find your way around such a big book, little groups of one or two sentences have been numbered, and then groups of those sentences have been collected into chapters.

So how do you find the one or two sentences that you want in the Bible? Let's say you want to find Matthew 5:5,6. That means you need to look in the book called Matthew, in chapter number 5 and verses 5 and 6.

You can find Matthew in the list of books at the front of the Bible. This tells you which page Matthew starts on. When you have turned to the beginning of Matthew you then search for chapter 5. Look down the page until you see the numbers 5 and 6. Those are the sentences (or verses) that you need.

When you do your Bible reading, try to spend a few extra minutes praying and worshipping. Praying is talking and listening to God. You can do this aloud or without using words. You can pray on your own or with friends. Worship is telling God how much you love him, through words or songs, or things you do. This can be singing in church, but it's a lot more than that. It's about enjoying the wonderful world God has made. It's about how we speak to each other. It's about how we live our lives.

As you pray you can:

thank God for his goodness and his help;

tell God how great he is, and that you love him;

ask God to help you, your friends, your family and other people.

If you are a helper using this book with someone who does not read, you will find guidance notes at the end.

The *Easy-to-Read Version* of the Bible is available to buy from Causeway Prospects.

David pleased God

1 King David

Then David died. He was buried in the City of David. David ruled Israel 40 years.
1 Kings 2:10,11 (Full reading 1 Kings 2:10,11)

This was written at the end of King David's life. David was the King of Israel for 40 years. That's a long time to be king! And he was a good king.

The Bible has lots to say about David. Only Jesus gets more space on the pages of the Bible than David. We can learn a lot from David's life – from the way he lived and the things he did.

David was a man of faith. He knew God and trusted God. Finding out more about David will help us to know God, too.

Dear God, thank you for King David, for his life and faith. Please help me to know you better. Amen.

2 Pleasing God

This is what God said about David: 'David, the son of Jesse, is a man who is like me in his thinking. He will do all the things I want him to do.'

Acts 13:22 (Full reading Acts 13:21,22)

David wanted the same things that God wanted. David listened to God, then did the things God said. That's why David pleased God.

As we find out more about David in this book, let's pray it will help us to please God more. Wouldn't it be good if God could say that you do all the things God wants you to do?

Dear God, help me to know what you want so I can please you. Amen.

3 David the boy

Then Samuel asked Jesse, 'Are these all the sons you have?' Jesse answered, 'No, I have another son – my youngest, but he is out taking care of the sheep.'
1 Samuel 16:11 (Full reading 1 Samuel 16:10,11)

Samuel went to see Jesse and asked to see his sons. There were eight of them, and David was the youngest. The Bible tells us David's older brothers were not very nice to him. It is sometimes hard to be the youngest child in the family. They can get bullied or left out.

Do you know someone who gets bullied? Or someone people are rude to? You could ask the people being nasty to stop, or tell someone else what's going on.

Dear God, please stop people being rude and bullying. Please help me to speak up when people are doing bad things. Amen.

4 David is chosen

Jesse sent someone to get his youngest son. This son was a good-looking, red-faced young man. He was very handsome. The Lord said to Samuel, 'Get up and anoint him. He is the one.'
1 Samuel 16:12 (Full reading 1 Samuel 16:11–13)

God sent Samuel to choose someone to be the next king of Israel. As soon as Samuel saw David, God said, 'This is the one. Anoint him.' Samuel put oil on David's head as a sign from God. This is anointing. God chose David to do a special job.

God still chooses people these days to do special jobs for him. God chooses ordinary people like you and me.

Father God, please show me what special job you want me to do. Please send your Holy Spirit to help me to do that work for you. Amen.

5 The shepherd

Then Samuel asked Jesse, 'Are these all the sons you have?' Jesse answered, 'No, I have another son – my youngest, but he is out taking care of the sheep.'

1 Samuel 16:11 (Full reading 1 Samuel 16:11)

David's job on the family farm was to look after the sheep. That meant going out with the sheep into the hills. David had to make sure the sheep had food to eat and water to drink. If a sheep got sick, David had to care for it and make it better.

Do you know anyone who works on a farm or who keeps animals at home? You could pray for them today.

Dear Lord, please help anyone looking after animals to do a good job. Amen.

6 Learning to fight

... David said to Saul, 'I ... was taking care of my father's sheep. A lion and a bear came and took a sheep from the flock. Each time I chased that wild animal. I attacked it and took the sheep from its mouth.'
1 Samuel 17:34,35 (Full reading 1 Samuel 17:34–36)

Being a shepherd was a dangerous job. David sometimes had to fight wild animals to keep the sheep safe. He learned to use a sling (to throw stones) and to fight with his hands.

Many people have jobs that can be dangerous. Firemen have to put fires out and rescue people from buildings.

In your prayers today, pray for firemen and ambulance men as they rescue and help people. Can you think of other people who have dangerous jobs?

7 The servant

Saul sent a message to Jesse. 'Let David stay and serve me. I like him very much.'
1 Samuel 16:22 (Full reading 1 Samuel 16:22,23)

At that time, the king was called Saul. David went to work in Saul's palace. David played the harp very well. That kept Saul calm when he was feeling unhappy. David worked in Saul's house as a servant.

Being a servant means helping other people. It means thinking about what other people need before thinking about your own needs. A servant makes other people happy by showing God's love to them. It's what God want us to do for others.

Dear God, please show me what I can do to serve other people and show your love to them. Amen.

8 David is ready

God chose David to be his special servant. David was caring for sheep, but God took him away from that job. God gave David the job of caring for his people ...

Psalm 78:70,71 (Full reading Psalm 78:70–72)

God was teaching David many things. As a shepherd, David learned how to care for sheep and people. He learned how to fight. In Saul's house, David learned how to be a servant. He also saw what being a king was like. Later on, God made use of all these things that David could do.

Think about the things you can do well. Thank God for them.

Dear God, please help me use my skills for you every day. Amen.

9 David and Goliath

The Philistines had a champion fighter named Goliath ... He was over 9 feet tall.
1 Samuel 17:4 (Full reading 1 Samuel 17:1–7)

Goliath was a giant – a great big man. He was the fiercest soldier in the Philistine army. The Philistines were the enemies of God's people, the Israelites. Nobody in the Israelite army dared to fight against Goliath. They were all too frightened.

David went out to fight Goliath and won. It is one of the best known stories in the Bible. David was young. He wasn't a trained soldier. But he won.

Wars are always bad news. People are hurt and killed. Homes and other places are spoiled. Families live in fear.

Think of a country where there is a war, and pray for that war to stop.

10 In God's name

David said to the Philistine (Goliath), 'You come to me using sword, spear, and javelin. The battle belongs to the Lord! And the Lord will help us defeat all of you Philistines.'
1 Samuel 17:45,47 (Full reading 1 Samuel 17:45–47)

Before David began to fight Goliath, he did something very important. First David said to Goliath, 'I come against you in the name of the Lord.' Then he said, 'The battle belongs to the Lord, and he will help us beat you.'

David was not bigger than Goliath. But David knew that God was bigger than Goliath. Whatever problems we have, God is bigger than the problems.

Dear God, thank you for showing me through the story of David and Goliath that you can do anything. Help me to trust you even when things look really bad. Amen.

11 Good company

Saul kept David with him from that day on. Saul did not let David go back home to his father.

1 Samuel 18:2 (Full reading 1 Samuel 18:1,2)

King Saul liked David. David played the harp well. He was good company. David was a good soldier and would do whatever King Saul asked. David was a good person to have around.

Do you know people like that? People who are good company make you feel better when they are there. They help everybody to be cheerful. They bring fun and laughter into a place.

Lord Jesus, thank you for my friends who are so good to be with. Help us to share fun and laughter together so we are good company for each other. Amen.

12 Friends

... Jonathan developed a strong bond with David. Jonathan loved David as much as he loved himself.

1 Samuel 18:1 (Full reading 1 Samuel 18:1–3)

While David was living at King Saul's palace, he got to know Saul's son Jonathan. They became really good friends. The Bible says Jonathan loved David, so it was a very close friendship, a special friendship.

You can have lots of friends, but it's good to have one or two special friends. They are people you can talk to about anything – even difficult things you don't talk to other people about. If they are Christians you can pray with them too.

Dear God, please help me to have a special friendship with at least one person. Help me to be a really good friend to them. Amen.

13 Sharing

Jonathan took off the coat he was wearing and gave it to David. Jonathan gave David his whole uniform – including his sword, and his bow, and even his belt.

1 Samuel 18:4 (Full reading 1 Samuel 18:1–4)

David and Jonathan were such good friends that Jonathan wanted to share some of his things with David. Jonathan gave David some of his clothes, his bow and his sword.

That's what good friends do. They give each other things to show how much they like and love each other. They don't have to be big or expensive presents. Things like chocolates or flowers will always be welcome and make your friend feel good.

Dear God, please help me to be good at giving, and to know what to give my friends. Amen.

14 Encouraging

... Saul's son Jonathan went to see David at Horesh. Jonathan helped David to have a stronger faith in God.

1 Samuel 23:16 (Full reading 1 Samuel 23:15,16)

There was a time when David was running away from Saul. Saul was trying to kill David, and David was afraid. Jonathan told David not to be afraid. Jonathan helped David to trust God to keep him safe.

Do you have a friend who needs encouraging? Someone who is afraid, or needs cheering up? Here are some things you could say to them:

- God knows all about it.
- God loves you.
- God is always with you.
- God can do anything.

Dear God, please send your Holy Spirit to help my friend. Amen.

15 Speaking up

Jonathan talked to his father Saul. Jonathan said good things about David.
1 Samuel 19:4 (Full reading 1 Samuel 19:4,5)

King Saul had fallen out with David. Saul was angry and wanted to kill David. So Jonathan went to speak to Saul. Jonathan said lots of good things about his friend David. Jonathan said that David had always been good to Saul and even risked his life for him.

What if people are talking about someone you know, but the things they are saying are not true? You can say, 'Just a minute! That's not true! Let me tell you what I know.'

Dear God, help me to know when to speak up for my friends, and to know what to say. Amen.

16 Making peace

Then Jonathan brought David to Saul. So David was with Saul like before.
1 Samuel 19:7 (Full reading 1 Samuel 19:6,7)

Jonathan spoke to Saul and told him good things about David. After that, Saul wanted to be friends with David again. So Jonathan brought David to Saul. David and Saul were friends again.

Sometimes friends argue or have a row, then refuse to talk to each other. What can you do? You can talk to your friends and tell each person good things about the other. Ask them to talk together. They might need to say sorry to each other.

Pray for any friends who have fallen out with each other. Ask God to show you how you could help them to be friends again.

17 A good soldier

Saul sent David to fight in many different battles. David was very successful. Then Saul put David in charge of the soldiers. This pleased everyone, even Saul's officers!

1 Samuel 18:5 (Full reading 1 Samuel 18:5,6)

King Saul put David in the army. He put David in charge of some soldiers. David was very good at it and his soldiers won all their battles. That made everyone happy. Saul was happy, the officers and soldiers in the army were happy.

When people do a good job it makes other people happy. Perhaps Jenny cooked a lovely meal. Maybe John organised a great day out to the seaside. Let's remember to say, 'Well done!' and 'Thank you' when people do things well.

Dear God, thank you for my friends who are so good at doing things. Amen.

18 Victory songs

The women sang, 'Saul has killed thousands of enemies, but David has killed tens of thousands!'

1 Samuel 18:7 (Full reading 1 Samuel 18:6,7)

David and his soldiers went out to fight the enemies of Israel. After they won the battle, they marched back home. The women sang songs about winning the battle – victory songs.

Do you remember David's words when he went to fight the giant Goliath? David said, 'The battle belongs to the Lord.' David knew that it is God who fights our battles for us. We should thank God when things go well.

We can use the words of this song as our prayer today:

No god is greater than you.
You are so faithful and true.
You help with all that we do.
No god is greater than you.

Amen.

19 Saul is angry

The women's song upset Saul and he became very angry. Saul thought, 'The women say David killed tens of thousands [of enemies]. And they say I killed only thousands [of enemies].'

1 Samuel 18:8 (Full reading 1 Samuel 18:6–9)

King Saul heard the songs the women were singing. That made him angry. The song made it sound as if David was a better soldier than Saul. Perhaps people would want to make David king instead of Saul.

Saul was upset and angry because David had done so well. People were pleased with David. Saul wanted people to be pleased with him! We call that jealousy. It's not nice.

Dear God, help me to be pleased when other people do well, and to tell them, 'Well done!' Amen.

20 A nasty attack

Saul threw the spear two times. But David jumped out of the way both times.
1 Samuel 18:11 (Full reading 1 Samuel 18:10,11)

Saul was jealous of David because he was doing so well. Saul was afraid of David, so he tried to kill him with a spear. David jumped out of the way and was not hurt.

Probably nobody will ever throw a spear at you! But sometimes people do things that hurt us. People can say nasty words that hurt our feelings. People get angry, might wave their arms or even hit us.

Do you know someone who says bad things or hits people? Think about them today when you pray.

Dear God, please stop people saying or doing bad things when they are angry. Give them your peace instead. Amen.

21 Running away

Saul tried to throw his spear into David's body and pin him to the wall. But David jumped out of the way. The spear missed David and stuck in the wall. That night, David ran away.
1 Samuel 19:10 (Full reading 1 Samuel 19:8–10)

The first time Saul tried to kill David, Jonathan spoke to Saul and David could go back to the palace. But today's part of the story shows that Saul tried to kill David again. This time David was so frightened he ran away and did not come back.

Some people just don't get along well. Whenever they talk, they argue. We say they seem to 'rub each other up the wrong way'. However hard one of them tries, it just doesn't work.

Father God, please send your Holy Spirit to help people to get on better. Amen.

22 In trouble

Saul took the 3,000 soldiers he had chosen from all over Israel. Saul and these men looked for David in the desert ... Night came. David ... went into Saul's camp. Saul was asleep ...

1 Samuel 26:2,7 (Full reading 1 Samuel 26:2,3,7,18)

For years Saul chased David. Saul had thousands of men, and Saul wanted to kill David. David kept running away and trusting God to keep him safe.

David had a chance to kill Saul, but he did not do it. God had told David he would be king one day. David was happy to wait for that day.

Sometimes we have to wait for God to show us the right time for something to happen.

God, please help me to be patient as I wait for you to answer my prayers. Amen.

23 King at last

God chose David to be his special servant ... God gave David the job of caring for his people ... And David led them with a pure heart. He led them very wisely.
Psalm 78:70–72 (Full reading Psalm 78:70–72)

God chose David to be king. But David had to wait a long time before God's word came true. But at last, after King Saul died, David became king.

David was known as a man who pleased God. David wanted the same things as God. Because of that he did a very good job as king.

Pray for Queen Elizabeth and for all of the royal family. Pray for the prime minister and his government. Pray that they will do the things God wants them to do so our country is a good place to live in.

24 Doing good

David said to Mephibosheth, 'Don't be afraid. I will be kind to you. I will do this because of your father Jonathan.'
2 Samuel 9:7 (Full reading 2 Samuel 9:6,7)

Do you remember that David had a really strong friendship with Jonathan, King Saul's son? David was king now, and both Saul and Jonathan were dead. Mephibosheth was Jonathan's son. David was kind to Mephibosheth because of his friendship with Jonathan.

It is always good to be kind to people. It is good to do things that make people feel better or solve a problem for them. It could be something as simple as talking to someone or praying with them.

Dear God, please help me to show kindness to someone today. Show me what people need to help them feel better. Amen.

25 Doing wrong

David sent messengers to go and bring Bathsheba to him. When she came to David, he had sexual relations with her. She ... then went back to her house.

2 Samuel 11:4 (Full reading 2 Samuel 11:4,5)

David was a good king, but he made mistakes. This was a bad mistake. He had sex with another man's wife. Then he made it worse by having the man killed. God sent a man called Nathan to tell David that God was cross about it.

God does not like it when we do bad things. The Bible calls them sins. Part of the Lord's Prayer says, 'Don't let us be tempted, but save us...' Let's pray that for ourselves today.

Dear Lord, please keep me from doing wrong things that make you sad and hurt other people. Amen.

26 Forgiven

God, scrub away my guilt. Wash away my sins, make me clean again! I know I sinned.
Psalm 51:2,3 (Full reading Psalm 51:1–4,10)

David knew he had done wrong. He was sorry about it. He asked God to forgive him.

We know that God can forgive the wrong things we do. When Jesus died on the cross he paid the price for all our sins. If we ask God to forgive us, he will forgive us. We will not be punished. Jesus was punished instead of us.

Is there anything you have done that might make God sad?

Father God, I am sorry for the things I have done or said that made you sad or hurt other people. Please forgive me. Help me not to do those things again. Amen.

27 David is upset

Then the king knew Absalom was dead. The king was very upset. He went up to the room over the gate and cried ... He was saying, 'O my son Absalom ... I wish I had died instead of you.'

2 Samuel 18:33 (Full reading 2 Samuel 18:32,33)

David's son was killed in a battle. When David heard this news he was very upset. He went away on his own and cried for a long time.

Grieving or being upset like this is normal. When someone who is close to us dies we feel very sad and upset. People who are grieving might need some time on their own. They might need time off work. They will need extra love and help while they grieve.

Dear God, help me show extra love to people who have lost a friend or someone in their family. Amen.

28 Life goes on

Then the king went to the city gate. The news spread that the king was at the gate. So all the people came to see the king.

2 Samuel 19:8 (Full reading 2 Samuel 19:8)

David was sad about the death of his son. He hid himself away and stayed on his own. But that stopped him doing his job. David's people needed him. So he decided he would get back to work.

It is right to grieve. We should help people to grieve properly. But we can't be sad forever. We will always remember the person who has died. But after a time we can begin to do everyday things again.

In your prayers today, think of anyone who is grieving. Pray that they will have happy thoughts of the person who has died.

29 Planning ahead

David had made plans for all parts of the temple. David gave those plans to Solomon.
1 Chronicles 28:12 (Full reading 1 Chronicles 28:11,12)

David had great plans for a temple (like a big church) in Jerusalem. The plans came from God. But God said that David was not the person to build it. David's son Solomon was going to build the temple.

God wants to tell his people (that's us!) about his plans. God has plans for each one of us – what we should do and when. Our job is to listen to what God says. Our next job is to do the thing God tells us about.

Dear God, please help me to know what plans you have for me. Help me to do everything well. Amen.

30 Forever

The Lord Jesus is the 'stone' that lives ... You also are like living stones. God is using you to build a spiritual temple. You are to serve God in that temple ...

1 Peter 2:4,5 (Full reading 1 Peter 2:4,5)

King Saul, King David, King Solomon – all of them died. Their kingdoms came to an end. But there is a King who is alive forever. That's Jesus! He will always be King and his kingdom will never end.

Solomon's temple was made of pieces of stone from the hillside. It did not last forever. The Church of Jesus Christ is made up of people like you and me. We are called 'living stones' in the Bible. Jesus' Church will last forever.

Dear God, thank you for Jesus. Help me to make a real difference whenever I meet together with your people. Amen.

Key words

Amen We usually say this at the end of prayers and it means, 'That's my prayer too'.

Anoint Pour oil on someone's head to show God has chosen them for a special job.

Battle When two armies fight each other, that's a battle. So if someone is having big problems, we might say they are in a battle.

Church Christian people together, or the place where they meet.

Faith Believing that God will keep his promises.

Forgive/ Forgiveness When you forgive someone who has hurt you you're not cross with them anymore.

Holy Spirit The Holy Spirit is a person. The Holy Spirit is God at work on the earth.

Jealous The bad feeling you get towards another person when you feel unhappy or cross that they are better than you, or you are worried that they will take your place or job.

Lord The one in charge. Another word for God.

Patient A patient person is happy to wait for things to happen.

Pray To talk to God or Jesus about things.

Servant Someone who does everything that another person wants them to.

Sexual relations The same as sexual intercourse, or having sex with someone.

Sin/ sins Things people do that make God sad and hurt other people.

Spiritual To do with the part inside people that helps them listen to God and do what he wants. It's about being a friend of God.

Trust Believing that someone will do what they say. Believing that someone can and will help you.

Worship Telling God how much you love him through words or songs or things you do.

Notes for carers and helpers

These Bible guides are designed to help a wide range of people who need extra help. It's impossible to tailor Bible notes to fit everyone's needs. But our hope is that many who have some level of visual or intellectual disability or just need a simpler approach can be helped to pray and read the Bible regularly through this series.

Some people will be able to use these notes without any help from others. But if you are the carer or helper of someone needing some assistance with using them, here are a few pointers which may be useful to you.

Before you begin, ask the Holy Spirit to help communicate the main thought from each reading and note to the person you are reading with. God through the Holy Spirit can communicate on levels that we cannot! Part of the Holy Spirit's role is to make Jesus real to people and you are working in partnership with him.

Make sure you have the person's full attention before starting to read. Think about how you can eliminate auditory or visual distractions in the environment such as TV or other people's conversations. Try to find a quiet place. Use eye contact to maintain good connection.

Read slowly and clearly, pausing where suitable. Facial expressions, hand and body movements can all help to underline the meaning of the material. Encourage whatever response is appropriate, particularly in prayer and praise.

Use your knowledge of the person to assess how much is being understood, how much clarification might be needed and how best to make applications more relevant.

Make your time together an opportunity for learning and fellowship for both of you.

Other titles in the Bible Prospects series:

Being like Jesus

Come, Holy Spirit!

God gives new life

In the beginning

Listen to Jesus!

Moses, man of God

Paul followed God

Songs of praise

The first Christians

The story of Christmas

The story of Easter